A COLLECTION
OF POETRY

VIOLET TENDENCIES

WRITTEN BY

Heidi Michelle

To my family, whose unwavering love and support are the roots of my strength. Your belief in me has been the melody that has carried me through every moment of doubt and triumph.

To my mentors, who illuminated my path not by dictating my steps, but by teaching me to find my way. Your wisdom and guidance have been the harmony that enriched my journey, allowing me to discover my voice.

To the rhythms of life and the symphony of human connections that inspire healing and growth. Your intricate notes have woven the fabric of my existence, infusing it with depth and meaning.

And finally, to the boundless passion for writing that has been my constant companion. Through the cadence of words, I have found solace, expression, and a bridge to others' hearts.

This book is a testament to the enduring power of love, the transformative nature of education, and the healing potential of creativity. May it resonate with you as deeply as the music and poetry within me.

Much Love, Heidi Michelle

Foreword

Violet Tendencies "is raw and unapologetic"

Violet Tendencies is a collection of powerful raw, poetry that delves deep into the human psyche. It explores the darker side of our emotions while bridging empathetic connections from our human experiences. Through vivid imagery and poignant words, this collection will take you on a journey through the tumultuous nature of your inner self.

I've experienced times of despair and hopelessness. Several years ago, my marriage was falling apart. There was infidelity, mistrust, hurt, pain, and shame. I accepted the shame as a way to grieve because I believed everything was my fault. Although we went to counseling and started to repair our relationship, I couldn't shake the hurt and it festered into subtle resentment. I was trying to hide my hurt and shame by acting as though everything was "good" when it wasn't.

For me, healing became possible after I sought out therapy and started to relinquish the shame that I had been harboring within my marriage. I began to work through the trauma I was experiencing and I indeed find hope in the Higher Power.

The poems in this collection are not for the faint of heart. They are raw and unapologetic, exposing the vulnerabilities and weaknesses that we often try to hide. But in doing so, they also offer a sense of catharsis and healing. Through the power of words, Heidi Michelle captures the intensity of these emotions and transforms them into something beautiful.

One of the most striking aspects of this collection is its ability to explore life in every stage of human experiences- like joy, love, sorrow, and acceptance, to name a few. It goes beyond the physical realm of feeling and delves into the subtleties of emotional and psychological experiences.

As I read through these poems, I couldn't help but feel captivated by the raw honesty and vulnerability on each page. Heidi Michelle's ability to evoke such powerful emotions is a testament to her skill and mastery of this artwork through photography and poetry.

Violet Tendencies is not just a collection of poems, it reflects our society and the human experience. It forces us to confront the uncomfortable truths about ourselves, the world we live in, and others we share it with. But it also offers a glimmer of hope, reminding us that even in our darkest moments, there is beauty to be found I want you, as the reader, to permit yourself to experience this book in a way that catapults you to healing and no longer hide behind your negative life experiences like I did.

I am honored to write this foreword for such a powerful and thought-provoking collection. I believe Violet Tendencies has the power to make a lasting impact on all of its readers, and I urge you to gift a copy to the people you love so they can experience this collection for themselves. Prepare to be moved and ultimately enlightened.

Shakira M. Releford, M.A.
Professor & Co-author of *Voices of Wellness Anthology*

Blurbs

In other's words...

"Every piece in this collection captivated me from start to finish. The raw, deeply relatable emotions guide you through profound journeys of self-discovery and healing. The title, 'Violet Tendencies,' immediately piqued my interest, and as I delved deeper into the text, I discovered how it seamlessly ties the entire work together. Each poem is a vivid fragment of emotion, creating a rich tapestry of experiences. But when I reached 'Violet Tendencies,' it beautifully wove these fragments into a harmonious whole, reflecting the author's essence.

The final piece lifts the curtain, allowing readers to witness the culmination of the author's journey and feel an intense, shared connection. This collection is a must-read for anyone eager to explore the depths of human connection and the transformative power of poetry. Don't miss out on this moving and unforgettable experience."

D. Alsibai Professor of Linguistics at the College of Language Sciences, KSU.

Violet Tendencies by Heidi Michelle reads like a secret diary of the author's most sacred hopes, dreams, and loves. As a music fanatic, I love how snippets of the song are seamlessly woven through the poetry, creating a flow and continuity to the work while exploring universally human topics such as love and loss, aging, sexual harassment, and religion. I truly appreciate Heidi's bravery in sharing her story. It's a book that will make you think and feel.

Chris Dean author of "Tales from a Broken Girl"

Violet Tendencies" - A Journey of Emotional Depths

Violet Tendencies is a collection that delves unflinchingly into the complexities of human emotions, offering evocative imagery throughout. "Lost In Emotion" wrestles with the blurred lines between love and confusion, asking poignant questions about healing and authenticity. The lines "Words used not with meaning left me alone and dreaming" encapsulate the ache of misunderstood intentions and the longing for connection. This poem sets a contemplative tone exploring themes of introspection and emotional vulnerability.

"Cry of the Phoenix" is a powerful metaphor for resilience and self-discovery. The invocation of the Phoenix's cry resonates symbolizing rebirth and transformation amidst brokenness. The poignant reflection "Never know who you are until you lose yourself in the people around you" invites readers into the journey towards self-understanding.

"Tentless Revival," is a phrase that echoes and serves as a poignant reminder that renewal and liberation from traditional structures and constraints is within all of us.

Jake Cutrer Minnesota ARC reviewer

Violent Tendencies by Heidi Michelle is a touching, straightforward collection of poems in sinuous rhymed couplets, with a few prose poems to boot. She employs simple, heartfelt language to explore deep concepts such as yearning, love, and relating to others. These poems are steeped in popular culture references. Many of her poems are irreverent, the clever wordplay embracing the contradictions in romance and faith. Violent Tendencies by Heidi Michelle is a book of honest, direct poems covering a wide spectrum of observations and emotions.

— Tony Brewer, author of Good Job, Lightning (Stubborn Mule Press)

Violet Tendencies is a collection of poems that seem to reflect the curiosity and musings

of a loner. A person who, on the one hand, longs to be seen and heard. "Blue Dreams"

explains that "I am still the unseen that didn't forget." At the same time, she displays a

level of confidence as shown in "Boots," where she says: "Before you piss me off and

bring out my claws, just know these boots are made for stompin' and one of these days

these boots are gonna stomp all over you." My favorite though, "Blind Farewell" is a journey of self-discovery. Though it starts with an outward view of the world, "We

all will love, and we all will die...", she realizes that she has

transformed and not the world around her. Self-realization comes into view in the title

poem "Violet Tendencies," where she grasps the reality of herself: "I tend to be violet,

like the flower, wild, curious, and full of power." This collection of poems presents a

multitude of moments of reflection, but together they are a journey through life

with revelations of self-discovery along the way. Violet Tendencies will draw you into

your journey of self-reflection, unhindered by experience and prior knowledge of

life.

Michael Carter

Lead Pastor, Author, Life Coach, and Speaker

www.michaelcarterspeaks.com

For me, *Violet Tendencies* explores universal themes with a modern twist. Reflections on such topics as grief, death, love, the workplace, and rock 'n roll contribute to the author's overarching theme of what it means to become more self-aware as we go through life. Each free-verse poem and prose vignette is a study of how the poet uncovered her own identity. Many of the poems include subtitles, another modern element, at least from my viewpoint. At first, the subtitles threw me a bit, but as I got used to them I realized they helped draw me into the message. Violets symbolize loyalty and faithfulness; Heidi Michelle is unwavering in her search for self.

~**Kerry Winderman, poet, educator, and author of** *The Dragonfly Chronicles*

Capturing personal introspection and broader societal themes can be a difficult dance and "Violet Tendencies" finds the interplay between them with nuance. The poet's voice is marked by a raw authenticity, diving deep into themes of identity, love, and resilience. Each poem invites readers into a reflective space where emotions are both explored and laid bare.

The strength of this collection lies in its ability to balance vulnerability with strength, offering experiences that are at once deeply personal and universally relatable. "Violet Tendencies" is a testament to the power of poetry to illuminate the human condition. As a member of our Bloomington poetry community, Heidi's contributions have always been heartfelt and thought-provoking. This collection is a beautiful extension of that same spirit

.-Dan "Sully" Sullivan, Author of *O Body*

HEIDI MICHELLE

Contents

Abscence

It's been far too long since I heard your song, the way
your voice rang in my ears.
Wistful and restless, my thoughts of you swirl, as purple
hues dance through my mind.
The thrill of the night, a cherished delight,
The scent of your cologne, the finest perfumes, a hint
of weed and alcohol consumed.

Your hair slicked back from your face,
I see your grin, your mischievous space.
Eyes like the ocean! Deep, endless, and full of chase.

Blue as the sky, encircling a pool, our gazes meet, and
I act like a fool.

Whether by chance or deliberate sight, our ears tune
to voices in the night.
Spinning fast and falling hard, we sing and shout with
no regard.
Time slips away, always too fast, what do we feel we
lack in the past?

A button to push, a chance to rewind, to relive those
stolen moments.
I'm addicted to you, just like a drug. When I go too long
without my high, I seek solace in the sky.
I search the stars to see your smile, the sound of your
voice drives me wild.
Pictures, videos, and memories are where you live, and
where you will be.

I eagerly await the next live date, wondering if it will
be the one where I meet my fate.
Waiting on you, what else can I do?
I live for the day, we are words away, while face to face
we seem.
I shake your hand and hug your arm, then place you in
my dreams.

A Way of Devotion

lost in emotion

It happened again; I got caught off guard.
A serving of pain and a dose of regard.
I want to see, just once to believe.
Do those flags that fly, glow red at night?
A Harmless plight, a hopeless dream.
I thought you were real, not just a scheme.
So fake and distasteful, my love was wasteful.
You don't deserve, or even have a chance, I would never give you a second glance.
I erase you, deface you, completely replace you, and move on.
Now I know not to trust, lest my heart shrivels, and turns to dust.
It's funny how we confuse love and lust, feelings, emotions, and super-less devotion.
We fade into a pointless motion.
Lost in love, or lost your head?

Which will heal and which will pretend?

Words used not with meaning left me alone and dreaming.

Lost and confused, left in a daze, you left me for the better days.

It happened again you stole my end,

You broke my heart that would not bend.

I gave you my heart and I told no lies, but

You lied and defied the rules of the beautiful mind.

Beautiful
Stranger

in the mirror

Imagine if you can a beautiful summer sun, and the splash of ocean waves hitting the rocks. The sand squishes between your toes, and the smell of coconut fills the air, the heat warming your arm.
Minding my own business, not trying to be seen, a gentleman walks by and says, "You're the most beautiful woman I've seen." Then he smiled and walked away.

Dream if you wish of a garden filled with blooms of every kind, tangled jungle vines wrapped down and around to a beautiful brook that bathes you in the finest fragrances unknown to man.

Your skin feels soft and supple, refined. Your hair lies like golden light swirls around your face, and you are dressed in white. You look at your reflection and the stranger says, "You look more than alright tonight." I blushed and giggled and thought, maybe he's right.

Walking down the sidewalk, I can sense a second heartbeat. It skips when I skip and swells joyfully when it is loved. This second heartbeat is so strong, I feel guilty, but I think I am in love!

As my eyes fall to a puddle on the ground, I see a light, the beautiful stranger has caught my eye. Bending on one knee to hear the stranger so clearly, "You are beautiful, loved, and blessed, don't you see?"

As I walked, my eyes filled with tears. I saw someone, a shadow smiling and waving in delight.

The smile that greeted me was my own! It was strange to me at first because I had never described myself or ever used the word BEAUTY.

What I saw was no longer a stranger but a reality that I finally allowed myself to believe.

Blind Farewell

In the fleeting time we are here, there will be many "Blind farewells."

There is a time and a season, and a reason for everything we do. We are born to die, urged to live fully, and always told to be careful. If we heed this advice, we contradict ourselves. We cannot live in fear and find joy.

"Blind farewells" are etched in time, with no warning, just a sigh, and another feeling of emotional lullabies.

We all will love, and we all will die. The question is, was your life just a long, slow, goodbye?

Just a thought and it might make you cry, but what if we never had to say goodbye?

Would it be for your good if your grandfather was always by your side?

Would it be fair to keep him alive while he silently suffers inside?

Would it be kind to love your accuser, and always forgive her, knowing she's a user?

You love her and hate to lose her, but you know it would be better if she were in a place where it doesn't make you feel like a loser.

A teacher of young now turned old, her "blind farewell" is the best story told.

She always laughed and smiled while she rode the train of unending blame, never knowing or showing her inner pain.

Graceful in flight, she flew like a dove, up to her father's arms, her first true love.

My "blind farewell" is to myself, and to the me I used to be.
I can no longer be the youngest version of me.
Time has taken my innocence, my energy, my love, and my sense of self.
I was blind, but now I see that growth is slowly encroaching upon me.
I will not be tamed or shamed for who I am or what I do, for you do not care for me, and I do not care for you.

Farewell to timidity and constricted voices.
For now, I am free to make and speak my own choices.
Adieu to thoughts that bind, you make me sick and lose my mind.
I form a new pattern in time that transforms the toxins that bind.

Goodbye at last to this little girl's past, now as me, I can sing and dance, slowly enjoying the romance.
When I put my arms around myself and softly whisper, I love you dear, I will look up in the mirror, and with a smile on my face, I recite a "blind farewell" to this bitter place.

Blue Dreams

are made of this...

Breath, the force of life and energy, flows with ease.
It requires no thought, an endless breeze.

Seeking the strange, ready to explore,
I lay down my worries, and let my spirit soar.

Overcome yet underwhelmed by life's tight frame,
I absolve and revolve, finding new ways to reclaim.

Hidden in shadows, in dark corners unseen,
Awaits a young dreamer, with an imaginative sheen.

Vitality blossoms, much like a dream,
In the mundane and insane, creativity streams.

Visions are now clear, clarity invites,
Reality sings songs of colorful lights.

Crashing waves of emotion rise high,
Despair turns to repair, under a starlit sky.

Exploration and ideas, swim to me from the sea,
Pathways unfold where dreams and moonbeams decree.

Voices speak in rhyme, free from time's bind,
My mind accepts the truth, imagination's find.
Feel the music, let it lead,
Embrace the rhythm, and set your creativity free.

Forget what's wrong or right, enjoy the night,
The sweet scents of childhood, and carnival delights.
Words spill out, shaking the ground,
No shame, no tears, only freedom unbound.

With love for humanity, there's so much to do,
Grief turns to hope, like morning dew.
Intense focus brings stillness, sharpens the skill,
Fading into dreams of blue skies, with a will.

Rainbows and roses snowflakes that land,
On the tip of our noses, dreams are grand.
Dream of the wild, the strange, the unseen,
Play your role, in life's vivid scene.

Climbing down from the heights, reluctant to leave,
Sweet freedom and softness, the sky we weave.
Back to earth, whether gently or with force,
I remain the unseen, following my course.

Light that brought vision, inspiration song,
Now I'm a soul where imagination belongs

Boots

are made for stompin'

I have a pair of black, knee-high combat boots, and one of these days, those boots are going to stomp all over you. I've had a couple of different pairs of these boots, a pair for each phase of my life when I needed them.

The first pair I bought at Hot Topic, I loved those boots—they went with everything, made me taller, kept me warm, and defended my honor more than a few times. I wore that first pair until I broke the zipper trying to still be a cool punk pregnant woman. Once I became a mom, I retired the boots. I kept them, but I did retire them. There's just something about a pair of shoes you've walked many miles in.

No more free-spirited lifestyle, no more doing what I want when I want, no more spending my paycheck down to the last dollar and not worrying, because it was just me. I had to be a polite adult now, a responsible mom and those boots were not well-liked by the "regular John."

My boots and I have been separated now for over 20 years, and I am proud to say that I finally bought another pair. The second generation of boots that asks, who can I kick now, what trouble can I flair? So, I proudly wore my new shiny black combat boots to my first rock show in years. I stood front and center, right at the rail, just to make sure the band could see my shiny new boots. I was having the time of my life, my boots and I were so happy and dancing, and then all of a sudden from behind, I felt a hand brush against me, I shot a dirty look at the guy behind me and told him to watch it!

I continued enjoying songs and went on with my night, my boots and I were still dancing, and I was still in heaven. Two songs later, it happened again. I felt the same hand. There is now a look I give to the band as if to say, "Hey, do you see this man and his hand?"

No one but me and my boots knew what to do, so with the next grab, I faced forward, held onto the rail in front of me, and with all my might, I did a swift kick back, right into the guy's sack of spite! I had such a great laugh, and I think the band did too! That handsy man didn't grab me anymore, in fact, the dude fell to the floor!

I love my boots even more. Over and over, you have protected me, loved my feet, and kept me warm. I know one day, like me, you too will be old and worn. So, let's enjoy the fuckery we cause, zip 'em up, and enjoy the show because we have so many more kicks to throw!

Although my boots decide the trouble I cause, I do try to be polite and pause... Before you piss me off and bring out my claws, just know these boots are made for stompin', and one of these days, these boots are gonna stomp all over you.

Celebrity

when you believe it in your head.

F ar beyond my dream, I search for my happiness. I lost it a long time ago.

I've heard all my life, "Why can't you just be happy?"

I don't know why I can't be happy; I don't know if I could tell you a time in my life when I was happy up to this point.

I've experienced "moments of joy" or exhilaration, both emotions that can fade when you leave. I heard a girl say the other day, "I don't want to go home to reality, that is so depressing." The reality for her was she would go back to not being special anymore, just another crazed fan like the rest of us. No one quite understood her fanaticism-jizm.

We can't all be rock stars or celebrities. Some of us have to be the fans. Some of us have to be the reality to wake others up from their unachievable, unrealistic, far-fetched ideas. Their actions are always to act first, forget the consequences, and maybe think about what they did later. I wish I could live free with no consequences because I might be happy.

What does that life look like when you are free to do whatever you please? What does it look like to have a job that you can only work a week a month, yet get paid like a boss and travel the world the other three weeks?

What if your job was to travel with a band and be the official photographer, journalist, or videographer? Sounds exciting, right? But I bet just like our jobs, they get tired of the same routine every night.

What would it be like to be that celebrity we all adore? Maybe you could live with all the perks, the constant attention to building your ego, every night people screaming your name, "We love you," through the distance of a crowded room. What a life to simply be adored.

The other side is that all you do is now public knowledge. Every move you make, every step you take, baby, they will be watching you. Every word that comes out of your mouth will be scrutinized and twisted by people you have never met.

You can say it does not bother you, and you don't read the hype, but something has gotten to you! I stand and watch as you slowly fall apart at night. Your self-destructive behavior, the drugs and alcohol to numb you. I understand a good time, but you always push past good and turn everything around you into complete chaos just because you like to fuck shit up.

Being a celebrity does not give you a right to be a dick to those who adore you and bow before you. We all need escapism, we need a break, and we want that one moment, to feel the energy of being a star and being loved by all.

Eventually, the gravity of reality is what knocks some sense into us, or causes us to dive deeper into our sins and continue to elude the kids, the man, and the gym.

As I sit and write about who I thought I wanted to be, I realize who I am. I may be just a fan in your eyes, but in my eyes, I shine brighter than you.

People who love me, love me because they know me, and not my celebrity.
I know if I lost everything material and was left with just me, I could start a fire in a mud puddle. What can you do but smile and dream?

Clinically Cynical in the Penta'cle

The Poem

Clinically cynical in the Penta'cle might seem obscene, but hey, religion and church aren't my scenes.

S ure, I believe in God and the divine, and I believe in myself, especially when I drink the wine.

Break the bread? In remembrance of those who formed my mind?

Born into a world that isn't mine, searching and stretching for boundaries to climb.

Cynical I am with doubt and disbelief. Is there a shepherd for all these sheep?

My love for humanity runs so deep, I empathize with the poor and oppressed, and yeah, I weep.

Why do we isolate and discommunicate the beautiful ones we don't understand? Why fear rules we can't comprehend?

Let's start by clarifying: clinical doesn't mean insane.

If I say I'm clinical, it means I can be efficient and stare at the rain.

I can be without feeling and still enjoy the sensation of pain.

I can be coldly detached, without love or shame.

Penta'cle, a sign of luck or magic? We're all shaped by tragedy. Add everything together, and here's what you'll see:

The lost and homeless, forced to live without.

People of all colors, disabilities, and clout.

All together in a clinical scene, rooms are empty, functional, and clean. Cynical it may seem to believe only what we see.

Naturally distrusting standards, raising our flag high with solemn lullabies.

Behind the Penta'cle, we hide, within a circle of pride. Magical scribes in sand passed from land to land.

Read, believe, and do as they demand. Future stakes for future fakes, you fools fall for a man. The Penta'cle was designed by a man with five fingers and toes, named Sam. The things we believe, the things we can't!

No room for doubt or disbelief, unless you want to be the Penta'cle thief. A talisman, a symbol of magic and mystery.

To hide behind the Penta'cle is to cover lies. Now, let's wrap it up and show you my hand.

The truest of showmen, I hope you understand that:

I am clinically, very cynical, for one with a Penta'cle in hand. If I speak to you, let my intention be true, from beginning to end, my friend.

Raised on clean, white, and functional, something feels cold, detached, and unemotional.

Seeking to feed and serve its own needs, making us swear loyalty
to be deceived. Acting as if they care, loving like they don't dare.
Cynical I seem because you are the destroyer of dreams.
Self-interest is the dish you serve to your queen.
Behind your cloak and jeans, your big bald head and endless
schemes.
My clinical cynicism behind the Penta'cle served me well in your
temple if I had to dwell.
So long, farewell, to the temple of Pew-die-pie.
Clinically cynical may seem unwell, but in this case, it worked like
a spell

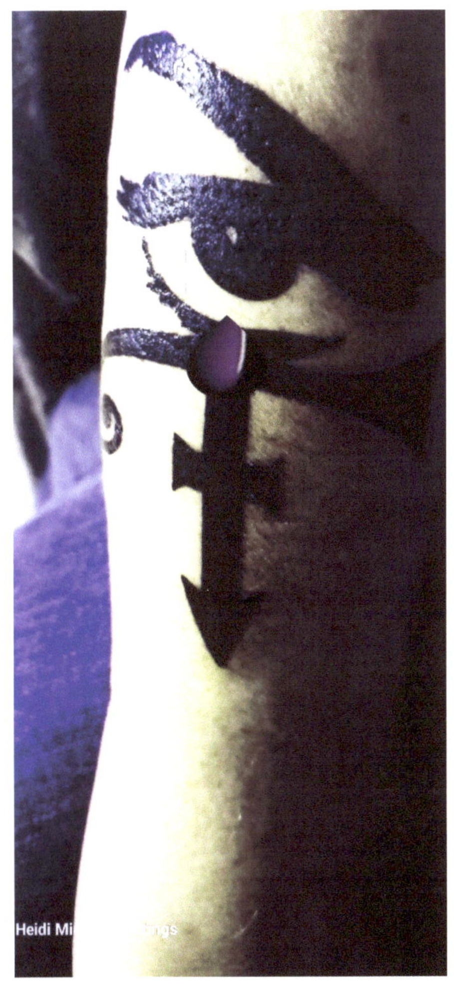

Cry of the Phoenix

Y ou left me standing here in such a cold, cold world.
Left me standing to carry the weight all on my own

Left me standing with my heart in my hand and face down on the floor.
Can you hear the cry of the Phoenix?
The cry of the broken, lost, and unclaimed.

Can you hear the cry of the Phoenix calling out your name?
Please, stop the blame!

She blames herself for being like her mother, never satisfied,
Always wanting more and always asking why.
She blames herself for not being more like her father, bold and unafraid,
But the emotional brain won't let her, she's tethered to her pain.

Never know who you are until you lose yourself in the people around you.
Who were you, who are you?
If you are lost after death, you will always fear the unknown that steers us.

Yes, you abandoned me, not once, but twice,
And now for the third and final time, and I weep,
For I know this is the last cry the Phoenix will cry,
For now, she must learn to fly alone in the sky.

Distance

I love you more than the distance that separates us,

More than the countless stars scattered across the sky.

I love you more than life itself,

And with you, every moment feels like the first time.

Our first kiss remains eternally sweet,

Each touch between us still carries its magic.

When you first whispered "I love you,"

It illuminated my world like a constellation in the night.

Love with you grows sweeter with each passing day,

As we explore new depths and embrace boundless pleasure.

Bound by our hearts, and the passage of time,

Our love story unfolds like a timeless fairy tale.

The way I love you may blind me to your flaws,

But it's this very imperfection that makes you mine.

You see me as bold and kind,

A discovery is both rare and divine.

In our tale of Beauty and the Beast, a mystery unfolds,

For the distance between us knows no boundaries

Deeper still..

Deeper still I want to know.
How the world spins and how the sun glows.
Deeper still to see a world that still believes in humanity.
Deeper still I need to know the me who hides deep below.
Behind the smile, below the radar, don't rock the boat,
seclusion, illusion, I relish in the delusion.
Fantasy swims throughout my head, what is real and what
is dead.
Visions and dreams I long to see, the truest version inside
of me.
Talents, gifts, and occasional blips, songs, and photogra-
phy.
I capture the vision and compose the symphony.
Mover closer to the end with thee.
Embrace the weird and obscene, and treat them like a
fantastic dream!

Dive right in and encounter, meet face-to-face, and enjoy
yourself.
Deeper still I need to know, what is life beyond my window.

Dream From Beyond

Awalk on the other side

In a scene that repeats like a haunting loop,
Crafted to ensnare, to terrorize and bewitch,
Leaving behind a hollow, tear-stained truth.

I see your face, worn and weathered by years,
Missing your smile, your radiant glow,
But most of all, our effortless flow.

White waves whip in the wind, lavender scent in the air,
Your smile now faded, no joy, no wild flair.
Your words fall on deaf ears, as you fade into light,
I awaken to find you lying there, gone from sight.

Heartbeat ceased, breath no longer there,
In your presence, in peace, a tear I dare.
Reality sinks in, irony to deal with,
Embracing the finality, what I truly feel.

I hold your cold, lifeless form for the last time,
Tears flow as I release you, ending your torment sub-

lime.
Blessing your spirit as rain fills the bowl,
Grief-stricken hands cling to memories, taking their toll.

Through darkness, the sun breaks, dispelling fears and

lies,
I begin to envision who I am, and where I rise.
A caterpillar transformed into a butterfly,
From loss to liberation, beneath the mourning sky.

Energy Vampire

In the eerie echoes of audacity,
In illusions that enchant and deceive,
Mind-numbing sensations leave spirits reeling.

Hope, courage, belief—all vanish,
Defiance stands, awe-inspiring, stark,
Bravery unfolds in a new, unsettling norm.

Courage breathes, fearless heartbeats,
Dancing jubilantly to an art unbridled,
A backbone forged in shattered dreams,
Sunlit hopes amid broken seams.

Legends of magic yet to unfold,
Energy vampires, torture untold,
Blinded eyes, words held in chains,
Feasting on cataclysmic pains.

Arrogance exploits, lies loom large,
Ruthless shoulders shrug, in charge.
Mysteries lost, wisdom hidden,
Secrets sleep with the haunted, unbidden.

Forbidden insights, illusions stark,
Darkness without light, shadows mark,
Haunted memories, lingering plight,
In the ghostly corridors of night

Family Reunion

Amidst another funeral, my eyes are bloodshot and my ankles are the size of watermelons from all these parades of mourning. Seriously, who invited Death to every party this year?

There's no chance to catch a breath, everywhere I turn, Death's got me on speed dial. I'm starting to wonder if I should just set up a revolving door at my place for all these mournful visits.

But wait, didn't I just swear off funerals two days ago? My self-control is as reliable as a chocolate teapot. Why is everyone I lean on suddenly playing hide-and-seek with the Grim Reaper?

Alright, Mr. Upstairs, we need to talk. You took Mom, my mentor, and my friends, and now you're burning both ends of my candle. Death and Destruction, you're like a bad houseguest who doesn't know when to leave.

Do you think you can strip us of everything? Think again. I'm the curse-breaker, baby. You exposed your cards, and now I know your game plan. Your reunion of doom ain't scaring me anymore.

Death, you're looking pretty wilted, like a salad left out in the sun too long. Your insults are about as effective as a soggy napkin at a picnic.

And hey, Destruction, you're just a big ol' drama queen. We're here, grieving and laughing and remembering the good times. You're losing your edge, buddy. We're turning your black cloud into a sparkly onyx ring.

So, Death and Destruction, take a backseat. We're the ones in charge here, raising a glass to our lost friends and saying, "See you on the other side, but not too soon!"

Fate Accompli

In the stillness of the night, I dreamt of you,
A vision is woven from longing and desire,
Your presence is a beacon, shining true,
Igniting passions that only love can inspire.

In my dreams, you are a deity divine,
Loved by all who kneel before your grace,
And I, a queen enchanted, wholly thine,
Adoring you in every tender embrace.

I dreamt of your touch, your voice, your taste,
Could you dwell forever in this heart of mine?
In dreams, our souls together interlace,
In a dance of love, where all is so fine.

Skin to skin, a sinful, sweet sensation,
Drawing nearer, our hearts entwine,
With each breath, a deeper dedication,
A union is pure, where love's tendrils entwine.

In years to come, what will our fate decree?
You, a god, and I, your eternal queen,
Bound in love's timeless tapestry,
A future bright, yet unseen

Fog of Nimit

Innocence gone

This is the most profound fog of all,
The Fog of Nimit is not a fault but a mindset.
An exquisite Utopia where we stand tall,
With no color, no hate, love freely met.

A smile, the secret to wishes we hold,
A laugh, the key to hearts intertwined.
The innocence of Nimit, pure and bold,
A rare gift, in this fog, truly defined.

In this fog, we live forevermore,
No cries for peace, no sounds of war.
I recall a friend named Nimit, so kind,
A genuine soul, no falsity in mind.

A peacemaker, a lover of all,
Yet not everyone could heed his call.
To make the world better, to see just a face,
Spreading love, peace, and joy in every place.

But the path of Nimit faced a cruel ploy,
His mission is marred by those who destroy.
The fog of Nimit, not of this land,
Exists in a space between far away and on demand.
Far Away could not grasp his love so pure,
For his home, not his land, his heart did endure.
When the fog returned to Far Away's grasp,
On-Demand exposed him to brutality's clasp.

The world watched, cruelty on display,
In an instant, the fog of Nimit swept away.
We stood revealed, a life meant to be,
Stripped bare, exposed to a harsh reality.

Far Away cared not, with thrashing might,
Leaving us bare, on the cruelest night.
Alone we weep through the sting of death,
Gasping for hope with each fleeting breath.

The Fog of Nimit is gone in form,
Yet he remains, urging us to reform.
Fear not the fog, nor the forlorn,
Maybe it's a chance to see humanity reborn

Full Forward

in front of my goal

I am full forward.

I am in front of my goal.

The waves pull me and toss me to and fro,

Yet I move toward the unseen, unafraid of what may be.

Watch me rise and soon become my dream.

I am moving forward, regardless of your beliefs.

If I followed you, I would be lost too, and that can never be.

You seek the reverse, living in a lie,

That is gone, no longer valid, destined to die.

Must you always try to re-write the lyrics to my song?

Attached as I may be, I am not for you, and you are not
for me.

I must move forward, progressing toward the love I
have for myself.

The path ahead is bright, full of possibility and light.

With each step, I grow stronger, ready to take flight.

No more looking back, no more dwelling on the past,

For my future is calling, and I'm moving fast.

I am unstoppable, driven by my fire,

Moving forward with all my heart's desire.

So watch me rise, watch me soar,

I am full forward, and I will be more

Identity

Do you know who you really are ?

Identity is mine, it is who I am, was, and am about to be.
Identity, I see you and me, I feel what you feel, but what is me?
I can be you, I can be me,
Yet, deep within, who am I truly meant to be?
I can change my style, the music in my head,
Even the sheets on my bed.
Identity, I see you and me.
I feel what you feel, but where is my clarity?
Identity, I've clung to everything that isn't me.
When will I feel free to simply be?
Can you morph into anyone? Can you change who you are?

Just to be a part of the crowd,
But what of the voice within, yearning to be loud?
Can you go unnoticed, like you never existed?
Do you scream inside for no one to hear?
Individuality, I see you and me.
I feel what you feel, but where is my true identity?
Identity, when will I feel free to be me?
I know what you do to try to manipulate me,
To feast on my energy, leaving me empty and dry.
But no more will I let my essence be denied.
Identity is mine, it is who I am, who I was,
And who I am about to be.
Identity, I see you and me,
Yet now, I embrace what is authentically me

Insatiable

i just can't get enough

I dream of your touch, the way it feels,

When your fingertips trace me from head to heels.

I yearn for you, for what could be,

A moment, just you and me.

A vision of us, sitting cheek to cheek,

Diving in without fear, our bond is unique.

I pray each night it's you I meet,

Until then, I am incomplete.

Love that knows no bounds,

A place where ecstasy and pleasure are found.

Sweaty palms and hearts that race,

Beating to the sound of our rhythmic pace.

Words so clever, and cavalier,

Your presence, oh so near.

I have loved you more, I have loved you best,

To me, you stand above all the rest.

I feel your gaze, sense you there,

As we share a moment, beyond compare.

Rest your head upon my chest,

In this embrace, find your rest.

Go with the flow, leave if you must,

But know my desire will never rust.

January Breath

A time to relax

I needed a fresh start, a clear path for the year,

January calls for resolutions, bold and sincere.

Arriving on the scene, I see my breath,

As I walk the pathway, embracing each step.

The air is cold, blistery, hard to inhale,

But time soon passes, and I feel strong and prevail.

A hug of emotion, a cup of tea,

An introduction to the new you and the new me.

Greetings proceed, stories are told,

Of the joyful, the fearless, the brave, and the bold.

We join hands, united we stand,

An unbroken circle, a powerful band.

Inhale the new hour, exhale the past,

No longer a time to sit and be an outcast.

Face your fears, make a throne of your enemy,

Embrace the power, let bravery be your legacy.

The air of the day, cold and bright,

Yet the fire within us shines like a lighthouse in the night.

Surrounded by white, shimmers of gold,

Purple and orange, shadows of old.

Some lay in bliss, smiling at rest,

While others weep, facing their tests.

Like a woman after labor, comes peace and calm,

We bask in the sun, singing a victorious psalm.

Gratitude, grace, relief on your face,

Burdens lifted, now move at your own pace.

Moving forward, waving back,

We swim in deep waters, it's our craft, our knack.

To be aware, connected, no fears, no regrets,

Living a life for the beauty it begets.

Light inside, fan the flame,

Time to rise, and reclaim your name.

January breathe, refresh, reclaim,

Embrace the difference, release the pain

Lost

Will you find a way?

I wish you the best above all else, I wish you happiness and health.

I have watched as you tore yourself down, and I built you back up.

You said you didn't need my help, but could not survive without me.

Here you come again, you're a wreck, I fixed you once, so what the heck?!

I offer you my all, and you take what you need to survive.

At times I am your sounding board for all the mistakes in your life.

What is sick is you always feel better after you have filled me with your venom, and left me in the corner of the room, alone to die.

You then ask me why I am so upset, and why I cry.
I cry for you because you do not want to change, you are satisfied with the tormented feeling of not belonging to this world.

I weep because the love I have for you is one you will never find again in your life.

You are the rock, that I fear may crush me, you are the strength I fear may strangle me, and you are the love I fear I will lose because we always lose the ones we love.

I agree, I deserve better, but time is of the essence, and I am creating a better life for myself.

My love, follow me on a journey beyond your mindset.

Feel the warmth of gold and violet rays fill your life.

Accept what you can change, and what you can not.
Be grateful for the time we have for I love with the power of 10,000 suns, but I love myself more than just the power of one.

My Favorite Band

has lost it's mind...

Sat by the ocean, feeling the cosmic waves roll,
Smooth sailing through dimensions, my mind's on a stroll.
My God is the sun, burning bright in my veins,
Daily I burn the witch, breaking all the chains.
No one here knows how to go with the flow,
Little sister, where's your shadow, in this neon glow?
Threes and sevens dancing in my head,
Losing my headache, and feeling good instead.
Feel good hit of the summer, echoing in my mind,
Misfit love on the rise, turning on the screw, one of a kind.
Vampire of memory and time, if I had a tail,
I'd blow your mind too, leaving no trail.
I'd be your monster in a parasol, never say never,
Always at your call, flying high forever.

Long slow goodbye, for now, feet don't fail me in this crowd,
Negative space dissolves, as the music gets loud.
I remember the night, my favorite band played,
Skin-on-skin obscenity, in my dreams they stayed.
If you believe it in your head, you know what I mean,
The band's rhythm is the psychedelic scene.
If you still don't know, I won't spell it out,
Live without the feel-good route, let the echoes shout.
Nicotine, Valium, Vicodin, Marijuana, Ecstasy, and Alcohol,
Through the haze, the music calls

My Lil' Blue

There's nothing I wouldn't do for my little one, my lil' blue.
Chase down the fears, and stare down the threats, I can't
let anyone drag you down, no regrets.

I love you more than words can convey,
In my every thought, both night and day.
Unconditional is how my heart feels,
Never changing, never yielding, steadfast, and real.

I'll always protect you, for that's what mothers do,
I see myself in the way you laugh, and in all that you pursue.
What would life be without my Lil' Blue?
Boring, dull, without your vibrant hues.

If I could, I'd always be around,
To see your smile and never a frown.

Your world is pure, lovely, silly, and kind,
In my life, such love is hard to find.
     You see the world as a fascinating mystery,
Eager to explore and uncover the secrets, full of history.
My Lil' Blue, I love you to the moon and stars,
Beyond the realms of dreams, beyond the farthest Mars.
     I could go on and on about the ways you shine,
Your silly songs, and facial expressions, are so divine.
Your willingness to learn and try new impressions,
Your big blue eyes are full of joyous confessions.
     You give no complaints, no need for praise,
My sweet Lil' Blue, in your innocent gaze.
You are my love, my joy, my bright yellow moon,
Forever and always, we'll sing our tune

Mystery to Me

Why you will never see...

If I had known, would I take it back?

I made my choice, can't look back now,

But my heart still aches, feels like a living hell,
With your screams and shrieks, echoes of past yells.

I remember the days when dining on your best hits,

Played so perfectly to the tune of "Unwell."

I sit and I stare, recalling the veil,

When I was yours, and you were mine,
But we blew it away and found different paths to tread.

Then you were us, and I was shut out,

Told I was hated, mostly just left out.

It's a mystery to me why we ever became

Just faces in the crowd, moving about,
Emotion gone, love turned out.

It's a mystery to me why I ever wanted to be
More than just me.
Time has passed, we've made amends,
But what if the future doesn't last?
You go back to you, I go back to me,
Each wondered if we were ever really sorry.

Did we mean the changes we fought to create?
Will we stay true to love, or succumb to hate?
If time is all we have and yet it's so short,
Why waste it on uninteresting words of retort?

It's a mystery why we try so hard
To get others to love us, to pursue,
When we owe them no due.
I send love to you, my son, despite the frustration,
For my love remains steadfast, through all tribulation.

Obstacle

Always in my way

Reached an itch I can't quite scratch,
An obstacle placed to test if the dreams I chase
Are worthy of the reward attached.

Learned now that truth unveils all lies,
The part of me that clings to fear must die.
Test me and watch me soar high!

Out of control, lost in the maze of my mind,
The part of me that seeks greatness
Navigate through hollows, sometimes blind.
Slipping back, feeling alone like stone.

As I stumble, you watch me fall,
Never there to answer my call.
The tragedy of our lives isn't in death's toll,
But in what we let wither within our soul.

I played your game, walked your path,
Endured your stick, your stain, your blame.
Through growth and pain, despite the strain,
The cost is less than bearing regret's chain.

Obstacles sapping my energy,
Reaching out to ensnare me.

Silenced, yet I found my voice,
Walked away, and made my choice.

Change's obstacle is tough at the start,

Chaotic in the middle, bursts into art.

Victims seek solace in amusement,
Victors embrace challenges and find improvement.

Choose wisely, for the obstacle ahead
May shape your fate, leave you misled

On The Rail

For the first time...

Everyone waits eagerly outside,
Seeking shade from the scorching heat.
Laughter and conversation, with a hint of weed,
Fill the air as we anticipate the beat.

The band rehearses, we join in on the verse,
Excitement building, anticipation terse.
Gates swing open wide, we rush inside,
First to arrive, racing to the stage with pride.

Hearts racing, eyes locked in focus,
Awaiting the moment, feeling so close.
Then, with a roar of delight and light so bright,
Queens of the Stone Age emerge into sight.

Screams of joy pierce the night,
We dance and sing under the stage's light.
Exhilaration fills the room, pure and intense,
Lost in music, lost in the moment's suspense.

Adrenaline rushes, veins alive with thrill,
Counting each second, time stands still.
In the night's embrace, under the pale moon,
We unite with the band, feeling in tune.

Obsession, devotion, pure emotion,
Linking our sounds in harmonic motion.
Pledging to rock and roll, to always be true,
Living in our shared obscenity, breaking through.

As the sunset hues paint the sky,
We walk to our cars, still buzzing high.
Memories of loud guitars, moments well spent,
Blissful hearts, not a single regret.

A night to remember, friends by our side,
In the echo of music, our spirits glide.
Rock and roll freedom, in the night we found,
A concert's magic, forever profound

Phoenix in December Remembered

In the depths of cold December nights,
We remember the Phoenix and her flights.
What have we learned from this journey of fire,
From ashes to rebirth, rising higher and higher?

The Phoenix, faithful to those she loves,
Rising from ashes, reborn from above.
A symbol of strength, revival, and grace,
A cycle of life, in each death a new embrace.

Love, fleeting yet profound,
Teaching us lessons, hearts unbound.
Grief and heartache knock on every door,
Yet love teaches us to hate no more.

We take new steps, changing our portrayals,
Speaking our truth, breaking through veils.
No longer disconnected, no longer alone,
In our acceptance, freedom we've known.

The wolf no longer haunts our dreams,
For now, it's the Phoenix that reigns supreme.
Lost beauty we seek in our dreams and our deeds,
In the love that grows from our deepest needs.

No more struggle, heads held high,
Wings aimed straight for the sky.
Let go of all that holds you back,
Embrace happiness, and keep your track.

Dream again, in the driver's seat,
Manifest your reality, and make your life complete.
Learn from defeats, rise from the fall,
Seize the day, stand tall.

Speak your truth, let no words be unspoken,
Cherish each moment, with hearts wide open.
Grateful for the journey, how far we've come,
From scars and burns to victory won.

My beautiful Phoenix, healed and whole,
Blessed with wisdom, a radiant soul.
Knowing the pain and victory's thrill,
In love, in life, finding peace and will.

Poison

Poison, creeping stealthily around,
Feel it in the earth, it's silent sound.
Green tendrils, like fungus, ever near,
Wrapping tight, feeding on fear.
Hands around your throat, tight and cold,
Leaving you adrift, lost in the fold.
Into the mist, forever to roam,
Breathing in poison, making you its home.
Drowning in fumes, sinking low,
Struggling to breathe, where shadows grow.
Clinging to hope, searching within,
Facing fears, where to begin?
Will I find you again, alive and free,
Or too late, lost to the poison's spree?
Poison fades, but leaves its stain,
Ashes to dust, in its domain.
Lying awake, thoughts consumed,
Knowing I shouldn't, yet still attuned.
Inhaling your poison, addicted to you,
Your touch, your feel, what you do.

Words of venom, no defense,
Enveloped in your intoxicating essence.
Mind poisoned, with shame entwined,
Caught in your game, a twisted bind.
Gripped by poison, held in place,
Strangled, choked, lost in disgrace.
Let go, release, break free from the grip,
Let poison take its final trip.
Lose yourself, in the quiet unwind,
Fear no more, what you can't find.
Peace, serenity, love divine,
Sleep now, till the end of time.

Purple Banana

the Purple One

Dearly beloved, today we gather to honor the Purple One,
A genius who made music matter, beyond compare, he shone.
Bold and ahead of his time, dancing with laughter and grace,

In his world of endless happiness, his sun is in every place.
"Dr. Everything will be alright," he'd muse about his mind,
Knowing time matters not when your spirit's unconfined.
De-elevator tried to bring him down, but he punched to higher ground,
Changing names, and worlds, leaving us begging for each sound.
With friends and love encircling, he wore a crown, adored by all,
Seeking Purple Bananas before they put us in that haul.
Some say we're crazy, a bit nuts, maybe bound for the yellow bus,
Yet in that whirl, we find meaning, why we're here, and what's for us.
Life's answer in that purple fruit, driving us wild, locking us away,
But for the Purple One, we'll love it until the end of the day.
Ride that elevator to the sky, shake, grind, let that voice wail,
In your purple and gold throne, know you were always dressed to prevail.
Beautiful, loved, forever blessed, Purple One, you outshone the rest.

RED

Not just a color...

Red hot like coals, I burn with anger ignited by you.

Not passion, but fury fueled by your games, untrue.

Pushing me beyond limits, binding me like chains,

Your lies are like smoking lips, echoing hell's refrains.

Silenced, expected to sit quietly, feeling small and ignored,

As insignificant as fleas on your hound, implored.

Clutching at me, a chain around my waist,

I bleed for your love, yet your heart remains encased.

Days pass devoid of devotion, emotions strained and frayed,

Strings tightening around my heart, hopelessly dismayed.

Left without fulfillment, needs to be left unmet,

Betrayed by your grip on the past, a painful regret.

No excuse for your use, your lies mere alibis,

I stand alone, awaiting your next cold reprise.

Shamed and isolated, lost in your callous tone,

Awaiting the day when regrets will be your own.

Caught in illusions, tangled in time's weave,

I bid farewell, no longer yours to deceive

Regardless

of how you feel...

Regardless of your feelings, I feel abandoned,
Lost in the wreckage you left, so coldly abandoned.
Wrapped in your self-absorption, blind to the pain,
Your lies reek of decay like a soul gone insane.
I wonder if you'll miss my touch, my voice in your ear,
Guiding you through the darkness, now that I'm not near.
Your flight has left me stranded, alone in the storm,
Empty, betrayed, believing in a false charm.
You took what was left of me, believing in your grand design,
Blinded by illusions, your reality is so unkind.
My resentment simmers, fueled by every rejection,
Growing stronger, a venomous infection.

We could have been beautiful, a love so true and rare,
But you squandered my kindness, left it tattered and bare.
Now I must move on, knowing I'll never have you,
For you offer nothing but pain, nothing but rue

Tentless Revival

inside my head

As a little girl, I remember "Revivals" Inside, outside, tent or no tent revivals. No one was dead or needed reviving, but it was what we did every year.

It was the week we all waited for, a committee was formed to plan for the revival. First, what was the theme? Something dynamic with a dash of flash, throw in some nonsecular music, a few speakers that could start fires in mud puddles, some free food, volunteers to occupy your kids with vacation Bible school during the night, just so the whole family can enjoy.

These are the simple steps to a tentless revival: As a girl, I had no voice, as a teen I had no choice, as an adult everything was my fault.

The 4 walls of the tentless revival could not hold me. The more knowledge I sought, the more I fought. Not just with myself, but also with those in charge of the circus. You ask, why would you describe it as a circus? Because it was an amazing showcase of talent and miraculous feats complete with a ringmaster we called Pastor.

It was the perfect illusion for those who were hurt, lonely, and secluded. Just like pigs to the slaughter, we were recruited to work for free and bring our family for some cookies and tea.

My tentless revival came one day when my head had a chance to clear. Red lights flashed like that reindeer we know, as I realized the lies as a child were damaged unseen. I now had a choice to shine without a theme. Tentless revival inside my head, now more like the Walking Dead.

The Calm and the Storm

Which are you?

orn to the tune of "Killing Me Softly" by Roberta Flack,
Yet my anthem was always "Stayin' Alive," never looking back.

Meant to be a ray of sunshine on cloudy days,

Singing blues away, kindness like a good hippie, my guiding phrase.

Blindly giving of myself, yet seeing the dark,

I embody both Calm and Storm, a solitary arc.

Growing into womanhood, my song turned "Delirious,"

Seeking peace in any form, fiercely independent and curious.

Stubbornly shaped by my inner child's whispers,

Disdain for liars and narcissists, moving mountains with fervor.

With maturation, eyes closed, seeing both dark and light,

Sunshine brings clarity, darkness conquers fears in the night.

Each year, not weaker but stronger I became,
No calm before the storm, it strikes without aim.
No peace in the storm's midst, no respite 'til the end,
For I am the Calm and the Storm, both foe and friend

Torch Her

Set her free...

Your grip is unseen, yet I feel the pull,

A rollercoaster of emotions, breaking me with every twist and twirl.

Confusion, frustration, hollow satisfaction,

Wounds salted, burning like fire, feeding your selfish attraction.

When will you release me from this endless plight?

Seeming to delight in keeping me enslaved, day and
night.

Torture echoes in my mind, threatening to unravel,

Chained by your unkind words, an endless battle to
travel.

You persist, thriving where there's no cure in sight,

How much more must I endure, trapped in this plight?

Your presence looms large, a shadow over me,

Yearning to escape the ride you designed, to break
free.

I try to flee, to find solace in hiding,

But the ache inside persists, with no respite in its
binding.

I wished you went, now here I stand alone,

Yet strangely, I miss you, your departure left a scar,
a place of your own.

Was I kind enough, despite your cruel ways?

I loved you deeply, you were my all, in the sun's gentle
rays.

My freedom came at a cost, a solitary grief to bear,

No one to blame, I sit with my loss, in silent despair.

I recall the person you once were, with fondness in my
heart,

Your smile, your laughter, the spark you ignited, now
a cherished part.

Amidst love's rise and fall, I move forward in my own
time and space,

Honoring your memory, finding peace in a new embrace.

Viewslides

Life's journey offers glimpses from diverse perspectives,
My stance remains clear and straightforward, with no direc-

tives.
A sprinkle of light, love, and a candid edge,
Yet today, as always, I ponder on life's ledge.

My concept of friendship diverges, it seems,
Acquaintance versus friend, not just in dreams.
Is it mere knowledge, or an in-depth bond?
Once past mere meetings, where do we respond?

Does familiarity birth casual friendship's gate?
Or does trust alone dictate our fate?
Extend my hand, met sometimes with disdain,
Rejected for not fitting the desired frame.

I can't fathom the lonely who shun nearness,
Or the perpetual anger, a cycle of bitterness.
Constant strife, perpetual ire, what a drain,
Spewing rage, relentless, always the same.

A pen to paper, venting anger's swell,
Art or rant, hard to discern, hard to tell.
Yet, I embrace diverse perspectives, I admit,
My visions mine, yours at time's summit.

I'll treasure the kaleidoscope life unfurls,
Hold fast to my essence, as the world swirls.

You keep your musings, at the edge of time,
While I cherish my truths, in the realm sublime.

Violet Tendencies

we all have them

Violet blooms wild, a subtle menace in the air,
Edible allure, timing precise with care.

Shared tendencies, desires loud and clear,
To be noticed, unseen deeds disappear.

World of violet hues, where the sun burns red,
Blue flowers cast shadows where roots are spread.

Retreat beckons from a callous world unkind,
Dreams of justice, heroics in mind.

Violet, violent, a single letter divides,
Beauty, brutality, where perception resides.

Once loved and trusted with abandon's art,
Now guarded boundaries, a shielded heart.

Red and blue blend in violet's embrace,
Love and sorrow in one harmonious place.

Violet, not just a flower, but a force untamed,
Curiosity and power, in its essence, claimed.

In my mind, a tempest may rage and seethe,
Yet tethered and grounded, I choose to breathe

Wanderlust

the need to explore

I wander, dreaming of a life so grand,
A thirst to roam, to travel, and to expand.

Curiosity drives me, I yearn to explore,
To meet faces unseen, and open new doors.

Wanderlust runs deep within my soul,
From Texas to Canada, I want to know it all.

Diverse cultures, experiences to seek,
Everyday adventures are thrilling and unique.

In my mind, fantasies take flight,
Cloaked in satin, pearls shining bright.

Parties with legends, both living and gone,
Prince, Hendrix, and Joplin, their music lives on.

But dreams blur into reality's gaze,
Where I stand, younger, in purple's embrace.

Crowds cheer as I wave, a fleeting goodbye,
Back to my world, where dreams can't die.

My job, my child, and my love's embrace,
I sing, write, create, finding solace and grace.

Yet the urge persists, the longing won't wane,
For music's allure, for a shot at fame.

I confess my wanderlust, my lustful dreams,
To travel, to sing, to dance in moonbeams.

Driven by passion, fueled by desire,
I chase the thrill, the spark, the fire.

When feeling stabby...

When I'm feeling stabby, it's like a drama scene,
In my head, you're a cutaway, a TV show dream.
I won't stab you, let's make that clear,
But in my mind, you're toast, that much is severe.
Stabby, oh stabby, just another emotion in play,
I tame it down and let it out when it behaves okay.
Then there's Mopey, like cheese toes in the heat,
Lacking motivation, smelling like a swampy retreat.
And Joy, oh delightful Joy, bright as the sun,
Playing dress-up, humming tunes, having fun.
Stabby, Mopey, and Joy, quite the trio, you see,
Giggling with toys, fighting battles silently.

When the day ends, Mopey takes the lead,
We fade with the sunset, fulfilling our needs.
Stabby's resting, feeling no pain,
But beware, call his name, he might come back again.

Acknowledgements
photo credits

Credit to Heidi Michelle Writings for the images for :

Absence, Beautiful Stranger, Boots, Energy Vampire, Family Reunion, Fate Acompli, Fog of Nimit, Full Forward, Identity, Insatiable, January Breath, My Favorite Band, My Lil Blue, Obstacle, On the Rail, Phoenix in December Remembered, Poison, Purple Banana, Red, the Calm and the Storm, Wanderlust, Lost, Tentless Revival, Masquerader, Torch Her, View slides, Violet Tendencies, Deeper Still, When Feeling Stabby, Celebrity, Clinically Cynical in the Pentac'le, Cry of the Phoenix and Dream from Beyond images.

Credit to D. Alsibai

Distance, Mystery to Me images.

About the author

Heidi Michelle is a passionate poet and writer whose work delves deep into human connection, self-discovery, and healing. With a unique voice that resonates with authenticity and vulnerability, Heidi Michelle has captivated readers with poignant reflections on life's most profound experiences.

Born with a love for music and an innate talent for storytelling, Heidi Michelle has always found solace and expression through the written word. Growing up in Southern Indiana, surrounded by the rhythms of daily life and the melodies of nature, Heidi Michelle developed a keen sensitivity to the world around her. This sensitivity is beautifully reflected in her poetry, which weaves together the complexities of human emotions into a tapestry of shared experiences.

Educated by mentors who believed in empowering their students to discover their paths, Heidi Michelle was encouraged to explore and nurture her creative spirit. This guidance has been instrumental in shaping the voice that readers have come to love. Heidi Michelle's poetry is not just a collection of words, but a journey—a journey that invites readers to explore themself and find healing in the process.

Violet Tendencies is Heidi Michelle's latest work, a collection that binds together vivid fragments of emotion into a harmonious whole. Each piece is a testament to the author's belief in the transformative power of poetry and the enduring connections that bind us all.

When not writing, Heidi Michelle can be found running off to concerts to see live music, reading at poetry clubs, writing short stories, and constantly learning about herself and the world around her. She currently resides in Southern Indiana where she continues to be inspired by the beauty of everyday life.

Also by

Other books by Heidi Michelle Writings

Phoenix in December by Scarlete Michele (aka Heidi Michelle Writings)

Originally released in December of 2023 on KDP as an e-book. Paperback January of 2024.

Phoenix in December takes you on a journey of an era in life that seems unsteady, and unsure of who you are meant to be. Relax and Enjoy the simplicity of just being!

9 7 9 8 3 3 0 3 6 9 9 6 6